Steam Trains

Paul Price

CHARTWELL BOOKS INC.

Designed and produced by
Albany Books
36 Park Street London W1Y 4DE

First published 1978

Published by Chartwell Books Inc.
A Division of Book Sales Inc.
110 Enterprise Avenue
Secaucus, New Jersey 07094

Acknowledgments

The publishers acknowledge permission to
reproduce photographs from the following
owners: Tom Bousted; Colourviews Picture
Library (J. B. Snell); Michael Holford
Library; Tony Hudson; K. Westcott Jones;
William MacQuitty; John Moore; Musée
Français du Chemin de Fer, Mulhouse;
National Railway Museum, York; Science
Museum, London; Spectrum Colour Library;
C. M. Whitehouse; ZEFA (R. Halin, G.
Mabbs, M. Pitner, L. Schranner).

Contents

The First Steam Trains

The first steam locomotive designed for railway use was produced in 1804 by the British engineer, Richard Trevithick. It was built to haul iron from Pennydarren to Glamorgan in Wales, but its five-tonne weight proved too much for the cast iron rails.

Other pioneers followed closely in Trevithick's wake, most notably George Stephenson (1781–1848), the first man to built a complete public railway. This was the 43-kilometre (27-mile) Stockton to Darlington Railway, authorized by Act of Parliament in 1821 to carry passengers as well as freight. The star of its inaugural run on 27th September 1825 was the engine *Locomotion* which, along with all the other components, was designed by Stephenson. Its feat on this first historic journey—hauling a coach full of distinguished guests, as well as over thirty wagons carrying railway workers, friends and merchandise—opened the Railway Age. After the first trip, however, locomotives were reserved for freight, and passengers continued to travel in horse-drawn coaches.

It fell to Goerge Stephenson's son Robert, who was destined to become world-famous as an inventive railway engineer, to create the first truly comprehensive "modern" railway. The Liverpool and Manchester Railway opened on 15th September 1830, having necessitated the building of a high viaduct and deep cuttings, each 18 metres (60 feet) long, as well as more than sixty bridges. It was the first public railway to be operated almost entirely by locomotives, and to have double track along its entire length. It was also the first to operate scheduled passenger services using vehicles and locomotives owned by the railway.

The engine used on the Liverpool and Manchester's inaugural run was the famous *Rocket*, which was

capable of speeds greater than 48 km/h (30 mph). The previous year, the *Rocket* had won the £500 first prize in the Rainhill Trials.

Among the illustrious guests on the first day, when eight trains left Liverpool for Manchester to the cheers of the assembled crowd, was the Duke of Wellington. While he enjoyed the ride, another guest, Liverpool member of parliament William Huskisson, was less fortunate. When the train stopped en route, he stepped off and was killed by a locomotive coming in the opposite direction, thus becoming the first railway passenger casualty.

Top: Locomotion *opened the world's first public railway, the Stockton & Darlington, in 1825. This working replica was built in 1975 for the event's 150th anniversary.*

Above: *an early French first-class coach of the Nord (Northern) railway in France (1850), preserved in the museum at Mulhouse, Alsace.*

Opposite: *George Stephenson's* Rocket *which opened the Liverpool & Manchester Railway in 1830 after winning the famous Rainhill Trials the previous year. Stephenson's concept and layout were to remain basically unchanged throughout the steam era.*

The Liverpool and Manchester was a great success. By the end of the 1830s Britain had around 2400 kilometres (1500 miles) of track compared with 150 kilometres (95 miles) at the beginning of the decade.

By the early 1840s, Britain had most of the features of a modern railway system—separate tracks for up-lines and down-lines, rails on wooden sleepers, a signalling system, passenger carriages with compartments, railway stations with waiting rooms and buffets, raised platforms and booking (ticket) offices.

How steam trains work

Thousands of different kinds of steam locomotives have been devised over the years, but they all operate in basically the same way.

Fuel (usually wood, although a wood and fuel oil mixture has also been used) is burned on a grate positioned at the bottom of the firebox. Flames and hot gases are given off into the firebox, and are drawn through a series of parallel tubes in the boiler into a smoke box at the front of the locomotive. The heat from the boiler tubes turns the water in the boiler into steam, which collects in a steam dome. The steam then passes into the cylinders by way of a regulator. There are usually two cylinders, one on each side of the locomotive. Steam, accumulated under pressure in the cylinder, drives a piston which, via a

Above right: Lion, *the 1838 Liverpool & Manchester locomotive that achieved fame through being used in the film* The Titfield Thunderbolt.

Above left: *a third-class dining car interior on the Great Northern Railway.*

Right: *impressions of trains at work on the pioneer Liverpool & Manchester Railway in 1831. In the picture on pages 6–7, it can be seen that the design of the last coach of the upper train derives from the contemporary stage coach.*

connecting rod and crank, turns the wheels. The exhaust steam then passes through the blast pipe in the smoke box and out through the funnel. At the same time it sets up a draught in the smoke box, which draws hot gases through the boiler tubes from the firebox. Using the regulator (or throttle), the driver controls the amount of steam which passes from the steam dome to the cylinder. He makes the locomotive go faster by increasing the amount of steam entering the cylinder, and slows it down by decreasing the amount. A safety valve is directly connected to the steam dome, and automatically releases excess steam if the pressure gets too high.

The battle of the gauges

Most of Britain's early railways were built to a gauge of 142·25 centimetres (4 feet 8 inches). This was the gauge advocated by the Stephensons, for no better reason, apparently, than that it was just about the width apart of the wheels on most road vehicles of the time.

Isambard Kingdom Brunel, who was the engineer of the Great Western Railway, built his line to a guage of 214 centimetres (7 feet $0\frac{1}{4}$ inches). This needed more land, wider bridges and tunnels, but it did allow for greater speed and roomier trains. The confusion which arose when standard gauge met broad gauge at Gloucester gave rise to the setting up of a Royal Commission, which in turn led to the Railway Gauge Act of 1846. The Act laid down that all railway track in England, Wales and Scotland was to be standard gauge (i.e. Stephenson's), with the one exception of the Great Western. Later this line conformed to the standard and the last of the broad gauge was converted in 1892.

Standardization did not, however, come to all other countries. In some, notably Australia, dif-ferent gauges in different areas still bedevil railway operations.

Railway Jubilee

By 1875, Britain was a veined mass of competing, connecting and overlapping railway lines. There were main lines, the pattern of which has not changed much to this day; and there were local and branch lines. The whole did provide some sort of national network, but in operating

Top: *Hungarian great-grandparent. Example of the bizarre 326 class of 1882 are still at work in parts of rural Hungary.*

Above: *in recent years the metre-gauge lines of Portugal have remained a haven for 19th-century steam. Here a fine old German-built tank locomotive is seen at Sernada da Vouga.*

Right: *the working replica of Germany's first locomotive (1835) Der Adler ("The Eagle" in the Nuremberg Transport Museum. Like many early locomotives that worked in Europe this was built in Britain.*

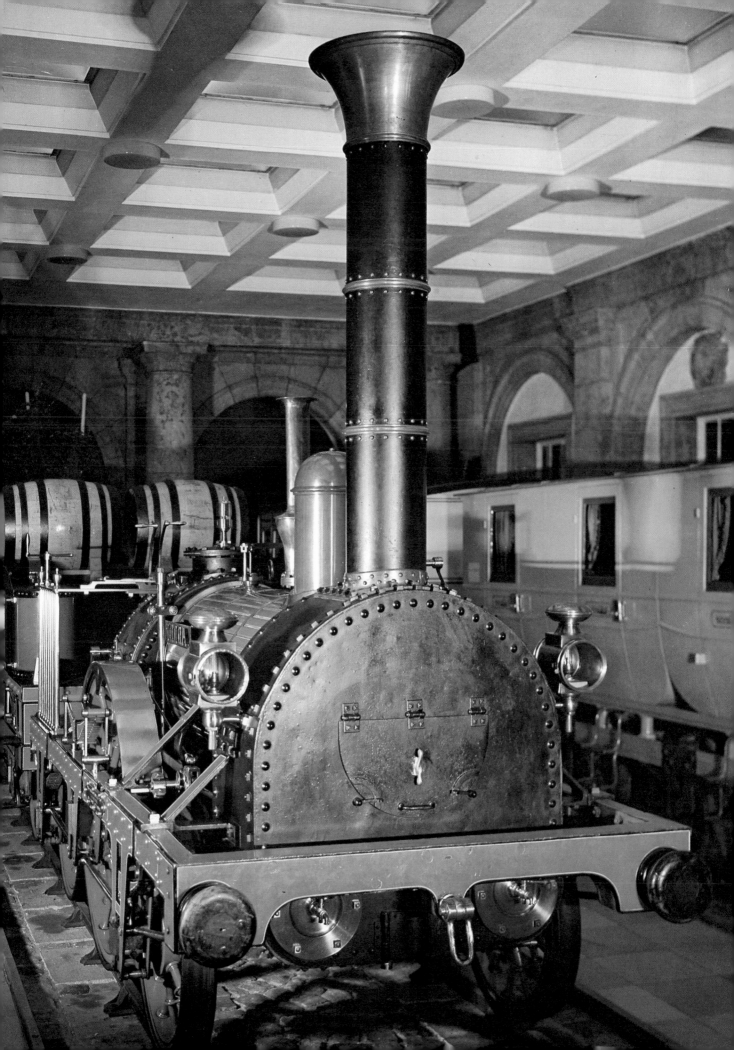

terms, it was very much broken up into a large number of separate companies. It was now possible, for example, to travel from one end of the country to the other by rail, but several changes had to be made on the way.

By now a number of standard developments were in general use. These included block-system signalling, which ensured that only one train at a time was allowed onto the stretch of line between one signal box and another; travelling post offices facilitated the sorting of mail on the move; rail-sea-rail links smoothed the way of cross-Channel passengers (the transit docks and steam packets usually belonged to the operating railway company). In addition, improved vehicle suspension provided a safer and more com-

fortable journey; and there were such refinements as heated carriages, refreshment facilities and sleeping berths.

All this time, the steam locomotive remained essentially the same beast as had been produced by the pioneers. But it was constantly evolving into the sizes and shapes which in most respects set the pattern for the years to come. While the *Rocket* had had a single pair of driving wheels, the norm was now two to four pairs of heavy wheels coupled together. The driver and the fireman now had a cab to give them shelter; and the tender containing coal and water, which trailed immediately behind the footplate, was (in the case of long-distance express locomotives) almost as long again as the main body of the

Above: George Sholto *on the narrow gauge railway at Bressingham, Norfolk.*

Above right: *the Khedive's Special of the Egyptian Government Railways.*

Right: *the Folkestone Express at Charing Cross Station, London.*

Overleaf: *preserved Midland Railway "Spinner" single wheeler No. 118 built at Derby Works in 1899.*

locomotive.

Although an average speed of around 65 km/h (40 mph) was considered sufficient for most journeys, trains were now beginning to reach 100–110 km/h (60–70 mph) in occasional bursts. The era of speed rivalry lay ahead.

The Khedive's Special.
Egyptian Government Railways.

Top: *North Wales is known for its narrow-gauge mountain railways. This is a Fairlie type locomotive of the Festiniog Railway, Earl of Merioneth.*

Left: *a branch line scene in Java, Indonesia.*

Above: *an Indonesian antique. A Beyer Peacock tram engine of 1884 still at work on the Surabaja tramway, Java.*

Long distance
and Luxury

The most impressive development in the last quarter of the 19th century was the growth of international, long-distance expresses, and the degree of comfort and luxury provided for passengers.

The pioneer of luxury rail travel was the American, George Pullman. In the 1860s, he introduced the first purpose-built sleeping cars, which were convertible for daytime use as parlours, saloons or dining cars. Pullman's sleeping car was adapted and taken up by other countries, but his day coach was transplanted directly from North America into several European railway systems. Its inventor's name was associated with this luxurious form of rail travel until the breed became virtually extinct in the 1960s.

With the advent of refinements, including washing facilities, equal to those provided by hotels and ships, the scene was set for the introduction of rail journeys lasting several days. There were, however, two obstacles to be overcome.

The railway operators in adjacent countries were reluctant to accept on their lines rolling stock belonging to someone else. There was also the technical difficulty of coupling together and hauling trains which, in many vital respects (such as braking systems, buffer alignment and general dimensions), were far from standard.

It fell to a Belgian, Georges Nagelmackers, to find an acceptable formula, and the financial backing to put it into effect. Inspired by Pullman, his idea was to form a company which would design and acquire a number of passenger coaches, equipped, furnished and staffed specifically for this kind of international journey. Each country's railway operators would continue to be responsible for hauling and operating these coaches within their own territories. They would be paid for the service pro-

vided from the proceeds of ticket sales and the revenue from mail-carrying contracts. The company formed by Nagelmackers became one of the most famous names in railway history—La Compagnie Internationale des Wagons-Lits et des Grands Exprès Européens.

At first, the coaches were four-wheelers less than 9 metres (30 feet) long. Each had a centrally placed washroom which connected with three compartments to be used as

Top: *a Soviet Su class mixed-traffic engine on the Trans-Siberian railway at Irkutsk en route for Vladivostok. The protective railings round the footplate are essential in the icy conditions of Siberia.*

Above: *a Garratt locomotive, effectively two locomotives powered by a single boiler, nearing Victoria Falls on the Rhodesian Railways.*

Opposite above: *Northbound express of the London & North Western Railway hauled by Webb compound locomotive.*

Opposite below: *busy morning at Oban, West Highland Railway in 1910, with two Caledonian Railway trains waiting to depart.*

sitting rooms during the day and bedrooms at night. These early prototypes came into service on the Continent in 1872.

By 1876, Nagelmackers' fleet of sleeping cars had grown to more than fifty. In 1881, he ordered the first of his restaurant cars with accommodation for twelve customers, and with gas lighting, coal-fired cooking facilities and, from the beginning, a *haute-cuisine* menu. In 1883, his efforts culminated in the inaugural run of the most famous of all steam trains, the Orient Express. The journey from Paris to Constantinople (present-day Istanbul) was reduced to eighty-two hours. Six years later, the train covered the entire distance in less than seventy hours. According to *The Times*' correspondent, de Blowitz, who travelled on the inaugural run, the train was "a marvellous sight" comprising "two

sleeping cars, two vans for baggage and provisions, and a restaurant car".

Other innovative steps were being taken in Britain. Train-based tours had begun in 1841, when Thomas Cook conducted a trainload of people from Leicester to Loughborough for a day's outing. For a total charge of one shilling, it included a cricket match and a visit to a stately home. From this modest beginning international tourist developed with Thomas Cook opening the way for British holiday-makers to Europe, the Mediterranean and beyond.

Railways were revolutionizing the way of life of people everywhere. Seaside resorts were now within reach of everyone who could afford the rail fare. Newspapers printed overnight in London were read at breakfast tables in distant parts of the country next morning. Busi-

Above: *London–Brighton Express of 1900 behind Billington B2 Class No. 64* Norfolk.

Right: *this poster conveys the speed and luxur offered by Canadian Pacific on their trans-Canada route.*

nessmen and politicians were able to extend their range of contacts. Families separated by migration to the growing industrial cities were more easily reunited. Fresh food and other basic necessities of life were more efficiently and speedily distributed. And the better heeled could commute daily between a country home and an urban place of work.

The railways were a vivid symbol of expansion, efficiency and success. Railway managements and employees became an élite: it was every schoolboy's dream to drive a steam locomotive. Carriages and locomotives, painted in gorgeous liveries, were lovingly maintained and cleaned. As engines were normally worked by one crew, a pride of possession resulted, which was revealed in gleaming paintwork and brass.

Boat trains

Naturally, boat trains with their international clientele were important shop-windows. One of the notable pioneers, in terms of comfort and efficient operating, was the overnight Irish Mail which linked London with Dublin via Holyhead. But the fiercest competition was in southern England, with companies vying for the cream of the cross-Channel London–Paris traffic.

For a time, five different British railway companies each had their own connecting cross-Channel packets, and transit ports under their own management. The London, Chatham and Dover company worked the route via Dover and Calais; the South Eastern via Folkestone and Boulogne; the London, Brighton and South Coast via Newhaven and Dieppe; the London and South Western via Southampton and Le Havre; and the Great Western via Weymouth and Cherbourg. The ferries were usually
26

capable of twenty knots, but in heavy weather, in the Channel's short, sharp seas, the crossing could be far from pleasant.

The Royal Trains

Luxury had become a keynote of rail travel for those who could afford the first-class fare. The standard (in a greatly modified form) was set by the Royal Trains.

As early as 1842, Queen Victoria travelled from Windsor to Paddington Station, London, in a

Top: *London, Midland and Scottish 2-6-0 No. 6441.*

Above: *London, Midland and Scottish 4-6-0 No. 5231.*

Opposite above: *royal grandeur—Queen Victoria's drawing room in the London & North Western Railway's royal train, now in the National Railway Museum, York.*

Opposite below: *more royal grandeur—Queen Alexandra's bedroom in the same train.*

luxurious drawing room coach. The following year, a coach was provided for her in the Midlands, which was heated by a small boiler placed under the floor. In 1850, a saloon provided for the Queen by the Great Western Railway boasted the first train lavatory. A few years later, the London and North Western supplied two coaches (one for daytime and the other for night use) which were the first to be connected by the "bellows" gangway, a forerunner of the protected intercoach platform of corridor trains. In 1897, the Great Western Railway built the first train intended exclusively for royal use.

Meanwhile, Pullman's drawing room coaches were appearing on more and more British trains. For many years, the all-Pullman *Southern*

Belle, which ran non-stop between London and Brighton, was the ultimate in luxury travel.

By 1868, some 128,000 kilometres (80,000 miles) of line were in use in Europe. As the 19th century drew to a close, the Golden Age of Railways was at its peak. In Britain, the network was virtually complete, with more than 96,000 kilometres (60,000 miles) of first class railway; Germany had nearly 30,000 kilometres (20,000 miles); some way behind came the United States and France. The British companies competed vigorously, striving to offer higher speeds, better service, greater value, as well as more exciting routes and destinations. Although average speeds were still below 80 km/h (50 mph), it was becoming common for express trains to reach 110 km/h (70 mph).

Above: *a "heavily-armoured" trans-Siberian locomotive.*

Competition-speed and service

One of the greatest speed contests in Britain was the "Race to the North". In 1888, the journey from London to Edinburgh was being completed in 7½ hours, the average time being 8 hours. A few years later, with the opening of the Forth Bridge, north of Edinburgh, Aberdeen was brought within 10 hours' travelling time of London.

The real competition was between the groups of companies operating the east coast and west coast routes from London to Scotland. In 1885, the fastest train on the west coast route, carrying first, second and third class passengers, was completing the journey from London to Edinburgh in 10 hours. On the east coast route, the *Flying Scotsman*, carrying first and second class passengers, was doing the journey in only 9 hours. Another train on the same route, which left London 10 minutes after the *Flying Scotsman*, took 10 hours. The west coast route began to lose passengers, so a 9-hour service was introduced. The east coast promptly responded with an 8½-hour journey. On the very day the west coast got its time down to 8½ hours, the east coast introduced a service which took 30 minutes less. Six days later the west coast achieved 8 hours, and for the next few days times taken on both routes got shorter every day. Finally, the companies agreed that the east coast route took 7¾ hours, and the west coast route 8 hours.

On the Great Western system,

Above right: *Britain's famous A3 class Pacific No. 4472,* Flying Scotsman *on a Hull–Edinburgh excursion in 1969. At that time, she was fitted with a second tender to avoid the need for special water supplies on long trips.*

Above left: Flying Scotsman *in semi-retirement at Carnforth in 1977.*

Right: *two London & North Eastern engines in pre-war apple green livery,* Green Arrow *and* Flying Scotsman.

always in the forefront of railway progress, the London to Plymouth route became the focus of public interest. By 1906, the standard time for the non-stop run by the *Cornish Riviera Limited* was just 4 hours.

New York Central v. Pennsylvania

In the United States, great rivalry arose between the New York Central Railroad and the Pennsylvania Railroad for passenger traffic between New York and Chicago. In 1897, the New York Central introduced the *Lake Shore Limited*, a daily service which took 20 hours and used luxury Wagner cars. (Wagner was a great rival of Pullman's.) Until then, it had taken 24 hours to cover the 1450 kilometres (900 miles) between the two cities.

The Pennsylvania Railroad's answer was the equally luxurious *New Pennsylvania Limited*, which took 24 hours. Initially the competition was over luxury and service rather than speed—the mediocre track limited top speeds to 65–80 km/h (40–50 mph). In 1902, the New York Central introduced an even more sumptuous train, the *Twentieth Century Limited*. But on the very same day, their rival's *Pennsylvania Special* came into service. Both of these trains were richly furnished. The dining cars were equipped with

Above left: the splasher and brass nameplate of Hardwicke, *a London & North Western veteran that took part in the "Race to the North" in the 1880s.*

Right: a mixed train in the Scottish Highlands behind preserved Highland Railway Jones Goods class No. 103.

Above right: South Eastern & Chatham Railway class C locomotive on the Bluebell Railway, Sussex, one of Britain's pioneer preservation projects.

Far right: a French émigré. AK class Pacific of the Paris–Lyons–Mediterranean Railway, now at Carnforth, England.

Above: *one of several thousand German war
locomotives built from 1941 and scattered ove[r]
all of the standard-gauge railways of Europe.
This one is hard at work in Turkey.*

Left: *the most numerous European passenger
class was the Prussian P8, of which over 380[0]
were built from 1906. They went all over
Europe. This one is at work on the Romania[n]
Railways on the southern edge of Transylvan[ia].*

linen and silverware; the buffets h[ad]
facilities such as baths, smoki[ng]
room and barber's shop.

It was in 1905 that the two co[m]-
panies began to reduce their journ[ey]
times. The *Pennsylvania Special* g[ot]
down to 18 hours and claimed to [be]
the fastest long-distance train in t[he]
world. Its engineers' claim that [it]
touched 203 km/h (127 mph) ov[er]
one 5-kilometre (3-mile) stret[ch]
has been refuted by experts. T[he]
Twentieth Century Limited also got [its]
service down to 18 hours, and so [now]
it too was claiming to be the fast[est]
long-distance train in the world.

Famous Trains

For a great many people, steam trains represented romance and adventure, none more so than the famous "named" trains of years past.

The Golden Arrow

By 1929, the cross-Channel Weymouth to Cherbourg route had gone out of business. All the other rival services (see Chapter 2) had come under the management of the comprehensive Southern Railway. Now the ultimate in London to Paris, all-Pullman luxury was introduced—the *Golden Arrow*.

Special trains on the English and French sides of the Channel were linked by a ship reserved exclusively for the service. Instead of the usual port formalities, passport checks and ticket inspections were carried out at the city termini or in transit.

The timing of the service in both directions made it possible to take lunch in the French portion of the train: the 3-hour run between Paris and Calais was just enough to do justice to the high standard of

Above: a French Nord Railway Pacific No. 3.1192 built in 1936 to the 1908 Paris-Orleans design as modified by the great engineer André Chapelon.

Right: the last single-driver in service in Britain was Caledonian Railway No. 123, withdrawn in 1935 and subsequently restored to its original condition.

cuisine and impeccable service in which France's Nord Railway prided itself. The British part of the rail service, with its shorter run between London and Dover, was not to be outdone: champagne and smoked salmon sandwiches on the outward run; a full English tea with hot buttered toast and cream cakes on the homeward run. Given fair weather for the sea crossing, a journey on the *Golden Arrow* was a memorable experience. For anyone with a taste for luxury travel, there can have been no more enjoyable way of spending the seven hours or so it took.

Sadly, this great train runs no more. The *Night Ferry*, however, introduced in 1936, survives and does good business.

ORIENT EXPRESS
NEAR CONSTANTINOPL

The Orient Express

The year 1883 saw the inaugural run of what was, probably, the best known of all steam trains—the *Orient Express*. The brainchild of Georges Nagelmackers, the train initially travelled from Paris to Bucharest, the remainder of the journey to Constantinople being made by local steamship and train. The whole trip took 80 hours.

Six years later, in 1889, the *Orient Express* itself was making the whole journey, reducing the total travelling time to 70 hours.

The *Orient Express* was always a "special" train. Because of the distance it covered, the number of frontiers it crossed, the fact that its destination was the "mysterious" Asia Minor, it had an unequalled aura of glamour and intrigue in the popular imagination. Its passengers were thought to be rich and glamorous, or sinister (spies, smugglers and international intriguers). Books were written about it, and novelists used it as a setting (for example, Graham Greene's *Stamboul Train* and Agatha Christie's *Murder on*

the *Orient Express*). Certainly this glamorous train attracted its share of eccentric passengers—King Boris of Bulgaria indulged his passion for steam engines by insisting on taking over the controls in the cab, to the alarm of crew and passengers alike.

To travel on the *Orient Express* was a very expensive business. Nevertheless, passengers (mainly British and German) flocked to buy their tickets to Constantinople.

Because the Ottoman capital was markedly ill-equipped to cater for an invasion of tourists, it was necessary for Nagelmackers to build two hotels of his own—the Pera Palace and the Therapia Summer Palace —to accommodate them.

The Compagnie Internationale des Wagons-Lits and the Compagnie Internationale des Grands Hotels were carrying tourists to and accommodating them in more and more destinations. The Peninsular Express brought Egypt within six days of London, the final leg of the journey being made by steamship from Brindisi.

SIMPLON·ORIENT·EXPRESS

GRANDE BRETAGNE. FRANCE. SUISSE. ITALIE
SERBIE. CROATIE. SLOVENIE. BULGARIE
ROUMANIE. GRÈCE. TURQUIE. SYRIE

Above right: *a diplomatic courier with his sealed bag of despatches at the Orient Express.*

Right: *the crest and computer classification number on an Orient Express sleeping car of th Wagons-Lit Company.*

Far right: *the destination board on the Direct Orient Express. This famous train was finally withdrawn in 1977.*

38

Le Train Bleu

The *Blue Train* was the name which was given to Nagelmackers' prestigious Calais–Paris–Nice Express. Inaugurated in the same year (1883), this train was even more luxurious than the *Orient Express*. The watchwords were novelty and glamour. This service, designed to carry the rich, the fashionable and the famous to holidays on the Côte d'Azur, started for the British at Victoria Station in London. After a three-hour Channel crossing from Dover to Calais, where a portion of the *Blue Train* was waiting for them, they travelled on to Paris to meet up with carriages from Berlin, St Petersburg, Warsaw and Vienna. Then the fully-sized *Blue Train* bore them to Marseilles and finally Nice.

The Côte d'Azur was enormously fashionable and Queen Victoria regularly wintered in Nice. Soon Nice and Monte Carlo were rivals for the vast numbers of rich and aristocratic holiday-makers who poured in from all the major capitals of Europe on the *trains de luxe*. As in Constantinople, Nagelmackers provided a sumptuous hotel in Nice —the Riviera Palace.

Railways in India

At the turn of the century, the Germans built a railway from Constantinople to Basra on the Arabian Gulf. Now India became a tourist attraction for the British, encouraged by Thomas Cook and Sons' offer of a choice of rail tours (escorted) of the sub-continent. Accompanied by vast quantities of clothing and equip-

Above right: a Wagons-Lits Company poster of the 1930s.

Right: a locomotive awaits the off in the Khyber Pass.

Opposite: a typical scene on the Darjeeling-Himalaya Railway in northern India which, by means of loops and spirals, climbs 2000 metres (6600 feet) in 40 kilometres (25 miles).

ment, and a personal servant t
attend to their every need, th
travellers would progress aroun
the country in what sometim
amounted to mobile holiday hom
—on rails!

The attraction for many wa
hunting. Special mobile shootin
carriages were built and attache
to a train. Long treks on foot, i
search of the wild animals, wer
avoided. The shooting carriage
conveyed the hunters up siding
and branch lines right to the animal
lairs.

The Trans-Siberian Express

The first overland service betwee
western Europe and the Far Eas
the *Trans-Siberian International E
press* was unveiled by Nagelmacke
in Paris in 1900. Here was a trai
more luxurious even than anythin
Nagelmackers had created befor
There was a library, with books i
English, French, German an
Russian; a music room with a fu
sized grand piano; a hair-dressin
salon; a gymnasium, and even
chapel.

The route took the travelle
through Siberia and the Chines
province of Manchuria all the wa
to Peking on what one early travelle
called "an ambulant palace
luxury". The same man did, how
ever, complain of monotony an
climatic hazards on the Siberia
tundra in winter.

Nagelmackers built yet another
his hotels in Peking, and the rou
flourished until the outbreak
World War 1.

A glance at editions of Cook
Continental Timetable, even of
decade or two ago, shows the rout
of many famous Continental E
presses radiating out in all dire
tions, like the spokes of a whee
Even today, there are throug
coaches from the Hook of Hollan

Top: *first of the Great Western's historic
Castle class No. 4079,* Pendennis Castle, *on
its final run in England. This engine appeared
at the 1924 Empire Exhibition, took part in the
1948 Locomotive Exchanges, hauled one of the
last steam trains on the Western Region in
1967, and was exported to Australia in 1977.*
Centre: *final run of* Pendennis Castle.

Above: Leander, *one of the London,
Midland & Scottish Railway's Jubilee class
introduced in 1934, George V's Jubilee year.*

Opposite: *the cab of* Caerphilly Castle, *a
preserved Great Western class now in the
Science Museum, London. The driver's seat is
on the right.*

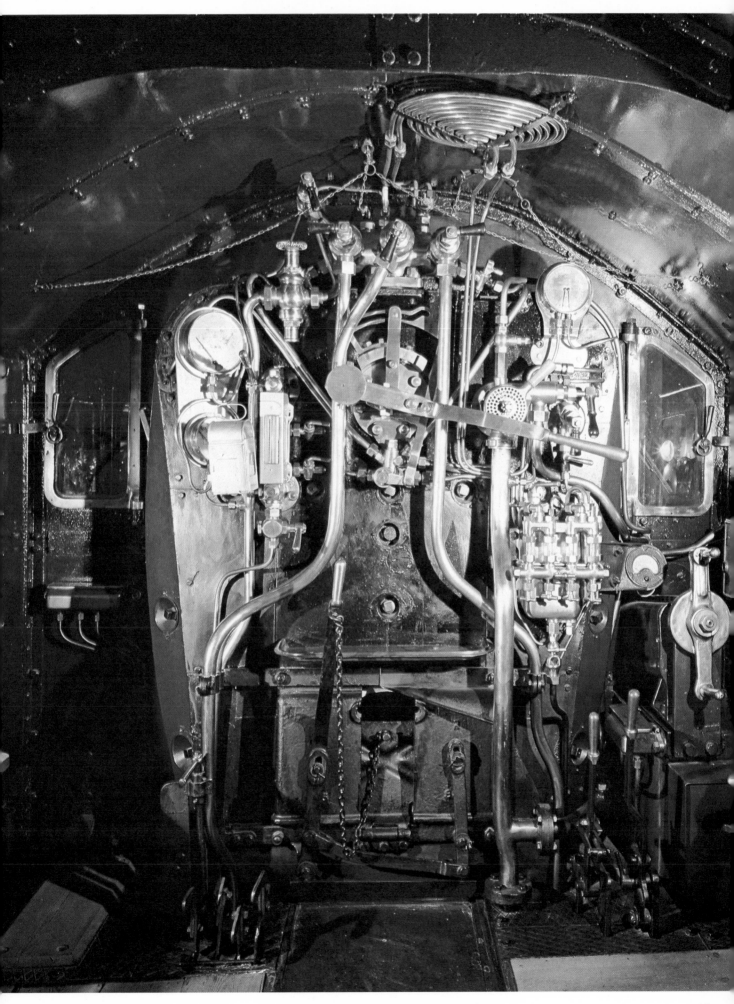

to Copenhagen, Berlin, Moscow, and, by means of the famous *Rhein-gold Express*, to West German, Swiss and Italian destinations. From Ostend, Calais, Boulogne and Dieppe, through services continue to run. Even though some are for the transportation of cars and their drivers, they are still trains travers-ing routes created for steam.

From Calais ran a portion of what became known as the *Direct-Orient Express*, as well as the famous *Rome Express*, which provided direct ac-cess to French, Swiss and Italian cities and resorts.

The *Malle des Indes* began life as early as 1855, carrying British mail to Marseilles, to be loaded there into ships bound for India, Australia and the Far East. In 1869, the train was extended to Brindisi, and from 1880, it carried passengers as well as

mail. As late as the 1930s, it was still running, as the *Bombay Express*, to Marseilles.

Another famous train, dating from 1887, was the *Sud Express* which linked Calais (and Paris) with Lisbon and Madrid. Connec-tions were provided with ocean liners calling at Lisbon and, by means of a change of trains in Madrid and a connecting ferry from Algeciras to Tangier, it was the main element in a schedule catering for the Morocco-bound European.

There is another *Blue Train*, one of the most luxurious overnight ex-presses, which links Cape Town and Johannesburg in South Africa.

In Australia, there is a service from Sydney to Perth, right across the country, where once the varying gauge meant a series of connecting trains.

The first Pacific class in Europe, No. 4546 of the Paris–Orléans Railway, 1908.

North American Trains

EMPLOYEES ARE WARNED
NOT TO GET ON
FOOT-BOARD WHEN ENGINE
IS APPROACHING

The first all-American locomotive, *Tom Thumb*, appeared in 1830 on a 20-kilometre (13-mile) stretch of line running out of Baltimore. In 1829, a steam locomotive had been imported from England by the Delaware and Hudson Railroad Company. It proved, however, too heavy for the track.

In January 1931, *Best Friend of Charlestown* began a regular service in South Carolina. This service ran well, until its fireman, in a careless moment, tampered with the safety valve and caused a violent explosion. In the same year, the Camden and Amboy opened its first section in New Jersey, and railway fever in North America began in earnest.

By the middle of the 19th century, the United States boasted 14,400 kilometres (9000 miles) of track. Although most of the lines were concentrated in the east, trunk lines were already stretching well into the mid-West, connecting New York with St Louis, Missouri; and Chicago was linked with the Gulf of Mexico in the south.

While European railways served on the whole to link long-established towns and cities, the American system was very much used as a way of "opening up" the continent. In many cases, the rigid civil engineering standards, which were observed across the Atlantic, were abandoned in the interests of speed of construction and minimizing cost. The European type of rigid short-wheelbase locomotive proved unsuitable for the American railroads, with their steep gradients and sharp curves. They were prone to frequent derailments.

The solution to the problem was found by John B. Jervis. He devised the 4-2-0. Built in New York in 1832, it was the world's first bogie locomotive. The front part was carried on a pivoted bogie which had four wheels. Thus equipped, the locomotive could take sharp

curves easily, and the longer wheel-base, giving three-point support, enabled it to travel twisting track without coming off the rails. Jervis' *Experiment* was the fastest locomotive of its day; at one point it covered 22 kilometres (14 miles) in 13 minutes—a speed of some 74 km/h (46 mph)!

From 1835 to 1841, two-thirds of all locomotives in service in the United States were 4-2-0s. In the 1840s, they were superceded by the 4-4-0, with three-point suspension, which was suitable for both freight trains and light passenger trains, and remained popular until the late 19th century. By 1870, nearly 85 per cent of American locomotives were 4-4-0s.

Early American Passenger Travel

Just as the European locomotive had proved unsuitable for the American railroads, so too did the rigid-frame European passenger coach. The first "bogie" carriage, where a long vehicle is carried on two independent bogies (or trucks), was introduced in 1831 by Ross Winans on the Baltimore and Ohio Railroad. The system had the advantage of allowing for a longer carriage.

Unlike the "compartmentalized" European passenger coach, the American interior was arranged as an open saloon with a central gangway. Less costly to build, these coaches could be heated effectively by a stove at each end. Steam heating was not introduced until the 1880s.

Left: *reconstruction of a typical 19th-century American locomotive at Tampa, Florida. The enormous chimney was designed to prevent sparks escaping, while the wooden cab protected the crew from the elements.*

Above: *the first locomotive on the west coast of the United States was the diminutive* Iron Horse, *now preserved in Oregon.*

47

The First Transcontinental

Although land was easy to come by, the approach to the West Coast involved construction work in wild and sparsely populated regions. Mountain ranges and rough low-lying ground added to the engineers' difficulties.

In 1862, after much wrangling and uncertainty, the United States government authorized the forming of two companies—one to work from the East, the other from the West—which would build the first line to cross the entire country. Some seven years later, the two sections met up in Utah. In May 1869, the last iron spike was ceremonially driven into the ground by Leland Stanford of the Central Pacific, which had started from California, and Thomas Durant of the Union Pacific, which worked from Omaha, Nebraska.

Technology

At about this time, American railroad engineers were making important technological advances. They devised the air-brake, which could bring the whole train to a halt by the application of a single brake in the locomotive's cab. A system of communications from place to place along the track, using morse code, improved safety and punctuality.

The Americans were also pioneers in luxury rail travel, through the inventiveness of such enterprising figures as George Pullman. His first sleeping car was introduced in 1865, and the ensuing rolling stock included sumptuous parlour cars for day travel. A few of these were available for private ownership, and, as status symbols, became almost as sought after as yachts. The most elegant, referred to as "mansions on rails", were nearly 30 metres (100 feet) long, extremely heavy and expensive (costing up to half a million dollars to

The "General" Made Famous by Andrews' Raiders Now on Exhibition at Union Depot, Chattanooga, Tenn. 141

acquire). Their embellishments could include open grates, printing presses, wine coolers, fine wood and glassware, as well as servants and live, milk-producing cattle.

By 1890, four routes were in operation across the United States. In Canada, the first equivalent east-west route had been completed in 1885. In both countries, the railroads promoted a sense of national unity among previously scattered and isolated communities, and

Top: *a famous old American, The General, captured by Captain Andrews during the Civil War in 1862.*

Above: *an early American freight engine preserved in Arizona.*

Opposite below: *luxury travel of a bygone age. The spacious interior of this old club car was possible thanks to the generous American loading gauge.*

Opposite above: *a transcontinental express i the Rocky Mountains of the Canadian Pacific Railroad in 1910. Note the cowcatcher, a prominent feature of early American trains.*

48

pened up new areas for develop-
ent and settlement.

Towards the end of the 19th
entury, American long-distance
xpresses were averaging about
5 km/h (40 mph), despite hazards,
ne of which is described in the
oxwell and Farrer Account of
889:

The entrance to many American
owns has to be traversed at very low
eeds as the railways are unfenced,
nning indeed in many cases along
e public roads, while intermediate
eed has often to be reduced where
railway is crossed on the level."

On the other hand, these re-
orters were pleased to note that
e *Overland Flyer*:

does the 1031 miles from Omaha
000 feet above sea level) to Ogden
301 feet) over two summits of
427 and 7395 feet (sinking to 6007
et between) at 29 mph inclusive
. of stops."

Europe, they said, this achieve-
ent would deserve a "laurel
own".

When it came to naming trains,
one was more inventive than the
mericans—more than 700 of them
ere promoted. Many reached
andards of comfort far superior to
nything available in other coun-
ies. A Boston–New York Express,
much as 70 years ago, offered
rivate staterooms, observation cars
rnished like club sitting rooms,
vo dining cars, and a travelling
aff of maids and porters.

Another élite route, well patro-
ized to this day, is that connect-
g New York with Washington.
ome of the leading trains on this
n continued south to Florida.
ew York–Chicago was also a pres-
ge route, which led to some of
orth America's most splendid
ains.

The Broadway Limited

Belonging to the Pennsylvania Railroad, the *Broadway Limited* leaves Chicago at cocktail time and arrives in New York at 9.30 the next morning. The train offers a lounge car with bar and a splendidly plush restaurant on wheels, complete with tail-coated maîtres d'hôtel. The traveller can retire after dinner to a private sitting room, and from there to a proper bed for the night. In the morning, a refreshing shower is available and, if wished, a full breakfast is brought to one's sitting room. A weather forecast and arrival information, specially printed on the journey, are pushed under the door. Telephone calls can be made from the moving train.

Twentieth Century Limited

Belonging to the New York Central Railroad, the *Twentieth Century Limited* was in its time America's greatest, most prestigious train. The New York Central system ran from New York to Chicago. It had been built up by Cornelius Vanderbilt from a number of small lines. Vanderbilt had tried and failed to acquire a monopoly of the route, which was intensely competitive (at one time there were eleven different routes serving the New York–Chicago link). Later it was the Pennsylvania Railroad, with its *Broadway Limited*, and the New York Central which competed for passengers.

The *Twentieth Century Limited* began to run in 1902. Its luxury set new standards for the forty-two passengers it could carry. Pullman built sleeping cars specially for the train. Although noted more for luxury than speed, it was covering the journey between New York and Chicago, a distance of 1450 kilometres (900 miles), in 18 hours. Steel cars replaced the old wooden ones, and the services offered were

onstantly being improved and added to. In the 1920s and '30s, the *Twentieth Century Limited* was at its height, and was advertised as "The Greatest Train in the World".

It was the New York Central, on this route, which gave American trains their characteristically "streamlined" look. This involved covering an existing locomotive with a steel shell, and was largely just a gimmick.

By 1938, the journey time was down to 16 hours, and completely new stock had been brought into service. After World War 2, through cars were attached to the train to serve Los Angeles and San Francisco. As air travel was adopted by more and more people, however, the heyday of the *Twentieth Century Limited* was past. The all-sleeper feature was abandoned in 1958. In the 1960s, the New York Central and the Pennsylvania joined forces in an effort to keep the service going. But unfortunately in 1967, it ceased to run.

The Canadian Pacific

The Canadian Pacific Railroad runs the longest continuous rail journey it is possible to make—from Montreal to Victoria, Vancouver Island. Strictly speaking, the last part of the journey is made by steamer down Burrard Inlet, British Columbia, to Victoria.

The Canadian Pacific came to be an integral part of journeys around the world. The sleeping cars were luxuriously furnished, with good ventilation and lighting. A favourite feature was the large picture windows, which gave splendid

Top: *a standard gauge Shay locomotive.*

Above: *a Heisler type articulated locomotive on the Cass scenic Railroad.*

Left: *Great Northern oil-fired Pacific No. 1246 preserved at Bellows Falls.*

views of the spectacular Canadian scenery.

The first CP passenger train ran on 4th July 1886. The service was, at first, rudimentary to say the least. But as with other famous rail services, standards were constantly being improved, until the degree of luxury and service equalled that of any other line.

The first passenger train to cross Canada ran in 1887.

Wagner, Pullman and Mann

While Georges Nagelmackers is the best-known figure in the story of European rail transport, there are three names inseparably linked with the American story.

George Mortimer Pullman's fame rested on providing luxury for rail passengers. In 1886, he introduced the first ever dining car, which he called the Delmonico. Although an important innovation, these early dining cars were far from satisfactory—for one thing the kitchen was in the middle of the car. It was some time before they came into widespread use, and generally meals continued to be eaten in buffets in stations. Pullman's name will always be associated with luxury travel. It must be said, however, that his reputation was largely founded on something less than the truth. Usually his cars were overcrowded, noisy and uncomfortable. Pullman was an expert publicist. Having started with a company manufacturing sleeping cars, he had a chequered business career. But his name will not be forgotten.

Wagner Company

The Wagner Company was a rival of Pullman's. Cornelius Vanderbilt put Wagner's cars on his Michigan Central line. A coach used by early New York–Chicago passengers belonged to the grandly named "Wag-

52

ner's Palace Drawing Room & Sleeping Car Line". When Wagner's sleeping car company and the New York Central got together, the result was the famous *Twentieth Century Limited*—noted for luxury and high-class service. Eventually the Wagner company was taken over by the Pullman company.

Above: *one of the last users of steam in the USA was the Denver & Rio Grande in Colorado. The silver paint on the smokeboxes of the locomotives was needed to withstand extreme temperatures caused by oil firing.*

Right: *a trio of Shays at Cass.*

Above right: *the world's largest steam locomotive is the Union Pacific's "Big Boy" Mallet type of 1944. Here, No. 4012 is in in retirement at Bellows Falls.*

Colonel Mann

Railway mania in North America was exploited by a great many people, not least a Colonel William d'Alton Mann. With a somewhat bizarre (and dubious) military and political career behind him, Colonel Mann got into the business of promoting railroad-building projects through the newspaper he owned in Mobile, Alabama.

Eventually he decided to set about building a railroad of his own—the New Orleans, Mobile and Chattanooga—which turned out to be a failure.

Mann then turned his attention to one-upping George Pullman, who was manufacturing rolling stock on a big scale. Mann called his carriages "boudoir cars". They were divided into compartments like European passenger cars, and were very luxuriously appointed. The trouble was they had room for only sixteen people. In fact, they were quite uneconomic, and American companies would not buy them. So Mann tried England.

Here he met up with Georges Nagelmackers, and the latter's Compagnie Internationale became a subsidiary of the Mann Boudoir Sleeping Car Company. (Pullman responded by forming the British Pullman Car Company.) Mann was extremely successful in Europe; Pullman was not. Eventually, however, Mann returned to New York and sold out to Pullman.

Above: *the Empire State Express.*

Technology

In the early days, British track was better aligned than American. To avoid steep gradients, large amounts of money were spent on cuttings, viaducts and tunnels, all of which meant the trains did not require to be so powerful.

Although 0-6-0s, 0-4-2s and 2-4-0s were in use in the late 1830s, they were mostly operated as goods engines. For fast passenger work the "single" (with only one pair of driving wheels) was widely used right up to the 1870s in the 4-2-2, 4-2-0, 2-2-0 and 2-2-2. Because the wrought-iron connecting rods were unreliable, it was not possible to produce locomotives with couple wheels which could safely travel at more than 65 km/h (40 mph).

The 4-4-0

A 4-4-0, rebuilt from a Norris 4-2-0, went into service on the Birmingham to Gloucester line in England in the late 1840s. In 1855, Daniel Gooch built a series of 4-4-0s with rigid wheelbase for the Great Western Railway. Five years later, Robert Stephenson & Co. built two-bogie 4-4-0s for the Stockton and Darlington Railway. In 1871, the typical British inside-cylinder, inside-frame 4-4-0s went into service on the North British Railway. When steel became available for wheels and connecting rods in the 1870s, the 4-4-0 became increasingly popular. Towards the end of the 19th century, most of the world's passenger trains were hauled by 4-4-0s.

Brakes

The only braking power on early trains was on the engine tender and on the guard's van. Early signals had to be very high, so that they could be seen by the driver from a great distance, allowing him enough time to bring his train to a halt.

Although a system of continuous

braking (in which all the carriages have their own brakes which can be applied simultaneously) was invented as early as the 1850s in Britain, *automatic* continuous brakes were not introduced until the 1870s. Automatic brakes are "fail-safe". They automatically apply themselves on both halves of a train if it breaks apart, or if the brake pipe is severed at any point along the train.

George Westinghouse's continuous automatic airbrake, using compressed air to apply brake power, was introduced in the United States in 1872-3. The British Gresham vacuum brake was introduced in 1878. Continuous automatic brakes were made compulsory in Britain in 1889 and in the United States in 1893.

Heavier trains

The invention of the continuous automatic braking system made it safe for trains to haul heavier loads at higher speeds. There was little

were called for, and there were a number of developments, including the enlargement of the boiler and the firebox.

The 4-6-0

The six coupled driving wheels of the 4-6-0 could support a larger boiler and so produce more steam. The world's first 4-6-0, the *Chesapeake*, was delivered to the Philadelphia and Reading Railroad in the United States by Norris in 1847. It was, however, twenty years before it achieved widespread popularity. By the end of the 19th century, it was the most common locomotive hauling mainline passenger services in the United States. The 4-6-0 passenger engines were not introduced into Britain until 1899, when the "S" class was put on by the North Eastern Railway.

The 4-4-2

The 4-4-2 had an extra pair of carrying wheels to cope with the enlarged firebox; the larger grate meant greater heat production. Although the first "Atlantic" type engine was built in 1888, the name was not applied to the 4-4-2 until the 1890s, when engines of this type were used on competing services from Philadelphia to Atlantic City. These were the first engines in the world regularly to attain an overall booked speed of 96 km/h (60 mph). Britain's first "Atlantic" type locomotive was built for the Great Northern Railway in 1898. It was later named *Henry Oakley* after the company's General Manager. The disadvantage of the "Atlantic" was that it had only four driving wheels, which caused difficulties on gradients, and it could not haul weights equal to those hauled by the 4-6-0.

The most successful of the passenger

Above: Sir Nigel Gresley's 100th express locomotive bore his name. The London & North Eastern A4 class streamliner No. 4498 was restored to its pre-war condition in 1977.

Top left: the Atlantic was the leading express type before the appearance of the Pacific in the first decade of the 20th century. This handsome example, No. 990, Henry Oakley, was designed for the Great Northern Railway by H. A. Ivatt.

Left: the Mallet locomotive has two sets of driving wheels articulated beneath a single boiler. It enabled powerful engines to be built for lightly-built and sharply-curved tracks. This Indonesian example was built in Switzerland in 1927.

Centre: a "chain" of locomotives.

demand for faster freight trains. There was considerable demand for faster passenger services. At the same time, rolling stock was becoming heavier as steel replaced wood in the construction of carriages, and passengers demanded greater comfort.

More power and more steam

locomotives was the "Pacific" type 4-6-2, which combined the larger boiler of the 4-6-0 and the extended firebox of the 4-4-2.

Sir Nigel Gresley's "A3" Pacific *Papyrus*, fitted with the Great Western Railway's improved valve gear design, averaged 128 km/h (80 mph), and reached a maximum speed of 173 km/h (108 mph) on a journey from London to Newcastle and back, hauling a 217-tonne test train. Three years later, one of Gresley's "A4" class Pacifics, christened *Mallard*, set a world speed record for steam of 204 km/h 126 mph) hauling a 204-tonne special train down a 1 in 200 gradient.

Superheating

Superheating was invented by the German engineer Wilhelm Schmidt, and was first used in Belgium in 1901. It was introduced in Britain in a Great Western 4-6-0. By the start of World War 1, it was being used for express passenger services in many parts of the world.

Steam from the dome is passed through U-shaped tubes inside the boiler tubes. This adds heat to the steam, which at the same time dries it out and greatly increases its volume. The superheated steam is then fed back to the cylinders, the efficiency of which is greatly increased by the rise in temperature.

Compounding

Compounding was successfully developed in France by De Glehn. There are two sets of cylinders in compound locomotives. First, steam is passed into high-pressure cylinders, which then exhaust into larger low-pressure cylinders. This meant that more power could be extracted from the same amount of steam. In Britain, compounding did not achieve widespread popularity. Also, it did not survive for long as new valve gear design was introduced, allowing steam to be got in and out of the cylinder quickly enough to make compounding unnecessary.

Above: *a Garratt of South African Railways standing on mixed-gauge trackwork at Estcourt, Natal.*

Top: *a typical British locomotive of the early 20th century, No. 1000 of the Midland Railway restored to its original condition. It is* compound, *that is the steam is used in two sets* cylinders *(high- and low-pressure respectively) before being expelled.*

The End of Steam

Rail travel today is faster, more efficient and more matter-of-fact. With the end of steam traction came also the end of the spirit of adventure and the glamour of rail travel. Now the steam train survives in a few private hands as an entertainment or a relic. Right to the last, its locomotive remained a vivid tribute to the engineer's art and skill. The final steam locomotive produced for British Railways was the *Evening Star*, a 2-10-0, completed at Swindon in 1960.

Steam trains disappeared from North America in 1960, from Britain in 1968 and from Australia in 1972. Scandinavia and western Europe have also turned to more modern forms of motive power. Steam does survive in less highly industrialized parts of the world, especially where labour and fuel are cheaper, for example South America, eastern Europe, South-East Asia, and parts of the Soviet Union and Africa. China is one of the few countries still building steam locomotives.

There are many reasons for the demise of the steam train. As a machine, its locomotive could not evolve and compete in efficiency with the electric motor and the internal combustion engine. With the need for a fireman as well as a driver, its operation became uneconomic in manpower terms.

Despite "every boy's ambition" to become an engine driver, and the pride which drivers and firemen took in their machines, the work was, by modern standards, heavy, dirty and uncomfortable. As functions, like cleaning and maintenance became more specialized and delegated to others, the sense of belonging between crew and locomotive was lost.

Primarily, however, the demise was a simple matter of comparative economics. The thermal efficiency of steam is very low compared with

Above: Evening Star.

Right: *one of the world's main users of steam power today is South Africa. Here is a 14 class loco of 1913 shunting coaches in Johannesburg in 1975.*

Far right: *Great Western Castle class No. 7029* Clun Castle *taking coal. This engine hauled the last steam passenger train out of Paddington Station, London.*

that of diesel and electricity. With the sudden rise in the price of coal in Europe and North America after World War 2, those other forms of traction proved to be more economic.